THE
GO-TO
GUY

The Life and Times of a Detroit-Area Mover,
Shaker, and Peacemaker

EDWARD DEEB

THE GO-TO GUY
THE LIFE AND TIMES OF A DETROIT-AREA
MOVER, SHAKER, AND PEACEMAKER

iUniverse books may be ordered through booksellers or by contacting:

iUniverse
1663 Liberty Drive
Bloomington, IN 47403
www.iuniverse.com
844-349-9409

Because of the dynamic nature of the Internet, any web addresses or links contained in this book may have changed since publication and may no longer be valid. The views expressed in this work are solely those of the author and do not necessarily reflect the views of the publisher, and the publisher hereby disclaims any responsibility for them.

Any people depicted in stock imagery provided by Getty Images are models, and such images are being used for illustrative purposes only. Certain stock imagery © Getty Images.

ISBN: 978-1-6632-1235-1 (sc)
ISBN: 978-1-6632-1236-8 (hc)
ISBN: 978-1-6632-1234-4 (e)

Library of Congress Control Number: 2021905302

Print information available on the last page.

iUniverse rev. date: 06/29/2022

Contents

Introduction

I am celebrating my 60th anniversary in 2020 managing important businesses and trade associations. My major at Michigan State University was journalism and advertising. It is a good thing because in the rest of my life, I am able to write and promote.

In the process of starting in my field, I began by being a copywriter in a small publishing company involved in the food industry to where I worked up from there managing several associations which helped solve various problems in the Detroit and Michigan area. When a problem occurred, I did not wait for people who didn't know what to do. I got on the phone and called the people to set up a meeting to help resolve the problem.

As a result, I began getting many calls from all over Michigan and other states and in Washington, D.C. who wanted to know how I resolved these problems. The more I did, the more calls I got.

I served as a member or officer of several community organizations and worked with so many people to resolve problems. I don't just talk about problems, I helped solve them.

I was getting calls from all parts of Michigan, and the major question they asked was how I got my information and was it factual. I have a personal rule never to put anything in writing unless it was accurate.

I also believe that talking was only the start of solving a problem. In the end, you had to meet with the people who had conflicts, sit down with them, and work out an arrangement where both parties accepted the solution you provided. This is probably the main reason I received so many plaudits and honors, which I never expected.

Training at MSU, being there on a 4-year music scholarship playing in both the Marching and Concert bands, I volunteered to assist various individuals and professors to eliminate any problems.

One of the honors I never expected was being asked by the Dean of the College of Communication Arts to become the founder of the school's Alumni Association and its first president. As a result, I played a key role in observing the new Comm Arts building that was going up and meeting with students and faculty to assure that we provided important subjects for them.

I could go on and on, but the point is, a problem cannot be solved by watching the opponents fight it out or talk on the telephone. It is resolved by taking charge and assuring that all parties want to resolve the problem and then actually resolving it. It takes more than just talking.

I am proud to have served in many non-profit organizations to help them achieve their goals. I have received many honors by these organizations for what I did, but I did not need to receive these honors in order to help bring the peace and tranquility and to get things done.

That's why they call me "The Go-To Guy".

– Edward Deeb

"The Power of Positivity and Talent—
The Ed Deeb Story"

Carol Cain
Emmy Award Winner, Producer, Host of "Michigan Matters"

Pioneer, Leader, Legend. Entrepreneur extraordinaire. You choose. As you read "The Go-To Guy" you will quickly ascertain all of those monikers (and more) fit.

Ed Deeb's impact on our city and region has spoken for itself for decades.

"The Go-To Guy" chronicles his incredible journey and provides significant insight into how one man, fueled with passion, determination, grace, and love, has done so much for so many.

From a purely personal perspective, I am beyond blessed to have witnessed firsthand, and reported on many of his accomplishments, yet, for those not as fortunate as yours truly to know this icon of a man, "The Go-To Guy" will tell you all you need to know about why few people will ever put their stamp on a community like he has.

"The Go-To Guy" is an exceptional read about the life and times of an exceptional man. Enjoy,

– Carol Cain

Foreword

Important to be Positive

By: John Prost
Grosse Pointe, Michigan

One may deal with a variety of different groups who may need assistance. Ed Deeb served on numerous boards of directors, along with various non-profit organizations such as Salvation Army and United Way as past chairman to mention a couple of many ... in the business, association, and charitable areas, not just one due to the many interests they represent. People working together matters. In the business and charitable fields, you still need a variety of different types of groups who need assistance.

Of the many organizations who requested assistance over the years, including several community leaders who wanted help asking why they have been stagnant or unable to become more successful than they were. They also discovered it was easier to work with smaller boards of directors consisting of 20 or less members due to the various interests, points of view organizations and who wanted to be more successful faster.

After Ed graduated MSU and served in the U.S. Air Force, he began learning about which groups are more likely to succeed and how he could assist them. These organizations played an important role (and still do) because they wanted to very much succeed and many long, hard hours were worked to assist many organizations or try to inspire them.

Ed has spent much of his time with groups such as Eastern Market (Detroit's farmers market), and major organizations in Michigan such as Michigan Food & Beverage Association, Michigan Business & Professional Association, Women and Leadership in the Workplace, Ascension-St. John Hospital, the Belle Isle Conservancy, Boy Scouts' Scouting for the Handicapped to name a few.

At the time his organization was encouraged by and worked with several supporters and helpers who had excellent association experience, such as Louis Vescio, Phil Lauri, Sal Ciaramitaro, and Harvey Weisberg, to name a few.

Journalists who helped along the way included Carol Cain, Dan Ponder, Paul W. Smith, Erik Smith, Neal Shine etc. from the Detroit area.

While various organizations were working hard to take care of their members, employees and support groups, our nation at many levels were trying to be successful peacemakers. Many nations in the world at the time were letting Deeb and his people know they have clout and wanted to be in the ballgame. No matter what the situation was, most nations wanted their moment of glory. They did their best to accommodate them and to be friendly as well. But tensions were high.

Today our nation is overwhelmed with a variety of problems or issues such as elections and candidates, political parties, opposing journalistic opinions, media publicity, a variety of controversial opinions from universities giving their differing views more often, terrorists shooting school children across the nation, terrorism involving our nation from the Middle East, Afghanistan, or elsewhere, tension currently involving China, North Korea, Iran, etc.

CORONAVIRUS – COVID 19

In March, 2020 our nation was hit with coronavirus. The disease trail went throughout the world, starting in China. Since then thousands of people died from this horrific disease, which the world has never seen such illness. Thousands were able to get treatment and able to survive and started wearing face masks.

Since then the United States and other nations organized massive networks of doctors, nurses, hospitals, and volunteers in various communities throughout our country and throughout the world and came together to fight the virus. Since the virus took effect many programs, sports events, auto races and various dinners had to be cancelled.

Even the important and colorful Metro Youth Day which is held on Belle isle in Detroit, the 38th annual, had to be canceled. This was the first time in 38 years it had to be cancelled. Our many sponsors and students who were to receive college scholarships were made aware of the cancelation. It is hopeful the event can be held in 2021 also at Belle Isle without needing to worry.

THE EARLY DAYS

IT **WAS** **IN** the late Forties in Detroit. The city and the nation had just rebounded from World War II and the great Depression. The Motor City was once again growing. People were working, buying houses. All was generally peaceful. Schools were excellent and students were graduating, finding jobs or going on to college.

Then in the 1950s and the early 1960s, Detroit became a more vibrant city. It continued to grow with few major problems. I attended elementary, intermediate, and Eastern High School there.

In these early days, we had very little problems in the community, the various high schools were eager to compete for high school championships, and there was more comradery between high schools as sports teams competed with each other.

Our family lived on the east side near Grand Blvd. and Mack Avenue. It was a friendly mixed neighborhood, a melting pot with different colors and ethnic groups—Italians, Syrians, Belgians, Irish, you name it. The kids were eager to play together. Little League Baseball had not started yet in Detroit, so the kids in the neighborhood got together, went to a local school playground, chose teams and played baseball without umpires or uniforms, Teams were evenly matched whether there were four to a team or ten, didn't matter so long as they had fun.

Dad worked at Ford Motor Company (later on started his own business) and mom was a typical homemaker and later worked for Michigan Bell. She raised three children: my brother Ray, sister Marge and me.

My time at Eastern High was challenging and interesting, with many things to do.

I began learning to play clarinet at seven years old. My parents insisted I practice every day. I couldn't go out and play baseball unless I practiced.

When I first entered high school I auditioned to play in the concert band. It was a great experience. All the clarinetists were quite good. There were frequent challenges to see who got first chair. We performed at various concerts and events.

My high school 1954 senior class had a special program held in their honor. Class officers decided to hold a little ceremony to honor graduating seniors. It was called: "This is Your Life," based on a popular early television program then hosted by Ralph Edwards.

Students were walking around wondering whose life would be picked. I sat next to the class president, Ted Theodorou, and said, "Ted, you're the class president I think they're going to pick you." I was surprised they picked me instead. It was a once-in-a-lifetime experience and honor.

They asked me to go upon stage and had a special program involving various classmates and teachers saying good or frustrating things about me. It was really an honor. I was nervous and overwhelmed.

This was in 1953. It was Senior Day and a chance to reminisce and think about our interesting past we had as students. The following January was graduation. We will be going into a new life after probably seeing some of our classmates for the last time unless they attended future reunions.

My folks wanted to give me a graduation present. Two weeks later I was in California visiting relatives. They were happy to see me and offered to tour the area. We even went south through San Diego and on to Tijuana, Mexico. Great experiences.

One of my relatives, cousin Joby Lewis ran a casino in Lake Tahoe just outside of Reno. The three-week trip was quite memorable. My first time really outside of the Detroit area.

We saw a lot of the flashing lights in Reno, and the various casinos and various sounds and music trying to attract visitors. It was so interesting to see all the activities of the area.

When I returned to Detroit I began working for Michigan Bell again during the day and helping at my parents' store in the evenings.

2

THE COLLEGIATE EXPERIENCE

FOR MOST OF us, high school was a great experience and a new beginning. After we graduated high school, many of us questioned what are we going to do next? Some wanted to go to college, some wanted to work and find a job, some wanted to take a vacation, and a few enlisted in the military. Many were thinking, will I go to college and where? What will the future be like? For me, the high school experience after school was helping my parents at their convenience store. Waiting on customers, filling orders, making sales, learning about the retail business and so on. It was a frustrating time for me and most of the graduates.

I then decided instead it was time for me to get a college education and develop something I'm interested in. So, I phoned Michigan State University in East Lansing and the University of Michigan in Ann Arbor and asked for an application to attend either school. I heard first from MSU.

Since I played clarinet, I asked the person if there was a chance I could play in the MSU marching band. She said that was not up to her, but to bring my clarinet and while at the university she would try to set up a meeting with me and the band director Leonard Falcone.

When I got there, the band director said he had some time and for me to go to the music building for a formal audition. Mr. Falcone greeted me and set three pieces of music in front of me for an audition ... one was easy, one medium and one difficult. After the audition he said to me I had done well in the audition and asked if I took private lessons. I said I did, and he asked who is your teacher. I said you might not know him since he is from Italy. His name was Alberto Luconi. Mr. Falcone was so pleased to hear that and stated it was his friend from Italy! So I was offered a four year college scholarship but had to play in the marching and concert bands. I was thrilled to hear that and told him I accepted the offer.

Band practice leading up to football Saturdays was 1 ½ hours daily and two hours every Wednesday night after supper. Most people and alumni loved to see the marching band perform. Practice was tiring but paid us dividends in the long run.

Bands then were notified that currently they were wearing the school colored uniforms, green and white. Just prior to the early fifties, band colors were military khaki colored uniforms. Everyone loved the green and white because it was more colorful.

When I attended State, we were fortunate that Oldsmobile Division of General Motors sponsored the band to all away games. We got to travel quite a bit and saw most of the other Big Ten colleges, getting to the campuses of Wisconsin, Illinois, Minnesota, Ohio State and Notre Dame to name some.

The band met each day at a coffee shop away from campus two weeks before we went to campus to practice music and formations for the band. Then one day I learned that a sophomore student, George Jacobs, was looking for me. Mr. Jacobs asked someone if a guy named Deeb was a member of the band. Someone answered, he was, but not here at the present time.

The next day, he heard I was at a particular dorm and asked the desk if I was in. He responded he just got back from band practice, and I'll tell him you're here.

Mr. Jacobs introduced himself and identified himself. Said he was from Buffalo, N.Y. and played the "derbeckee," a type of Arabic drum. Jacobs said he heard I once played some Middle Eastern music, and thought they could start an "Arabian" band on campus.

The two spent time practicing some music. Two other students, Tony Hattenback and Nat Sabal, who lived in the same dorm, had heard them and asked if they could join them. Tony played "maracas" and danced, while Nat played the "clavicos". During the session, Jacobs said he played Arabic music and the four of them would be a big hit on campus.

The next day after band practice, around 4 p.m., the group met again. Jacobs said the head of the MSU Student Council was holding a ceremony on the walkway at Spartan Stadium to introduce freshmen to the various student activities on campus. She told him "I heard you guys have a new band ... come over and play a couple of tunes." He responded they would try.

The four arrived at the stadium at around 6 p.m. and performed two numbers. The students loved the oriental sound. Unbeknownst to everyone, a Michigan State News photographer was present and took photos of the band. Surprise, the next day their pictured appeared on the front page of the State News. From that point on, several organizations began calling upon the new Arabian Knights band to perform at their sorority and fraternity parties.

The next thing that happened was that a freshman gal who lived in a dorm near the band's practice field sought me out and told me her dormitory wanted to "adopt" the band at Landon Hall. I said, "What do you do to adopt a band?" She responded, "we would like you guys to perform in front of our dorm every Wednesday evening. We will prepare new interesting costumes for you ... red and white necktie, red cuffs, and cumber bun, and black sandals with light socks showing through." You guys would look like real Arabs!"

The idea was presented to the band members. They thought it was a great idea, and performed every Wednesday night in front of the dorm.

The Arabian Knights band became quite popular after that. Most fraternities and sororities began having special Arabic-themed parties. The band lasted three years on campus, before George Jacobs left to get his Master's at another college out of state.

During their three years of existence, the group became so popular that even the marching band director wrote music for the group, and the band performed at halftime programs on the field.

On several occasions they were also picked to provide entertainment for guests of the MSU president John Hannah, and then Michigan Gov. G. Mennen Williams.

When I began my collegiate career at MSU, there were some 24,000 students totally who attended. The new College of Communication Arts and Sciences had only 46 and I was one of them. Today, the curriculum has more than 4,000 students in Comm Arts, and more than 50,000 students enrolled today.

Playing in the band away at other Big Ten universities as well as the concert band on campus for various occasions taught me the benefit of teamwork.

There were many things I picked up in college and learned how important it was for individuals to work together as a team, to get things accomplished, or you might call it sharing.

3

SERVING UNCLE SAM

WHEN I GRADUATED from MSU and received my degree, I did the normal thing – started looking for a job, hopefully in my field of study – communications, journalism, advertising, etc.

I landed a minor position as an assistant production manager with a food industry newspaper. I had to proofread stories, lay out pages and at times, write "fillers" to fill empty space.

During the early fifties and sixties, it was understood that young men could be drafted to serve in the U.S. Army or other branches.

During my second year at the job, I received my letter to report for active military duty. (I wondered if I would get my job back when I returned from service.)

I was eventually drafted into the U.S. Air Force and notified I needed to report to Lackland Air Force Base in San Antonio,

Texas within a week. So I flew to Lackland and became part of the original "Rainbow Flights", rainbow because the civilian clothes they wore to get there came in a variety of colors as in a rainbow. Shortly thereafter, they received their official Air Force uniforms.

As happens sometimes in life, after I began my tour at Lackland AFB, Texas, the first thing the Training Instructor did was to discuss duties of the new airmen including the area of marching. He lined all of us up, then chose the four tallest of us to be the squad leaders – one for each of the squads. I was chosen because not only was I one of the tallest, but because he also said we were good marchers.

He asked me "How did you learn to march?" I responded that my experience came through the MSU Marching Band. That seemed to please him.

I attended classes on base each morning. Then beginning our third week of training at Lackland, a Lieutenant Baker came into the classroom and asked if there was anyone in the squad who played musical instruments. There were six of us who responded "yes" including myself.

He excused us from the classroom, and led us into the hallway, then asked us what instruments we played. There was one who played piano, a bass player, a drummer, and myself being a clarinetist and played tenor sax.

He said to us we will be given some time each day to practice and learn some of the music. He said this coming Saturday, you guys would be the "dance band" which will perform at the outgoing general's retirement party in the Officers Club.

Come Saturday, we performed and I thought we did a pretty good job with only four days of practice.

The moral of this story is, you never know what you will be asked or ordered to do in the military. After 10 weeks of training at Lackland, members of our team were sent to different Bases. William (Bill) Summers and I were sent to cooking school at Ft. Lee, Virginia.

I had brought my clarinet with me to Ft. Lee thinking I would get a chance to practice. But I didn't have the time. It was a fairly new Selmer clarinet with silver keys. Expensive, so I didn't want to lose it.

During the second week at Ft. Lee, my group at the cooking school who manned the serving line, surprised me and placed a "cooking cap" on my head which read: "Chef Boy-Ar Deeb." I went along with it whenever we were in the serving line.

Fellow airman, Bill Summers, from Indiana, drove his car to the base after we were sent home for a week. Since I was from nearby Michigan (Detroit), he asked if I wanted to ride with him to our new base in Virginia. I responded that would be great and be able to see the countryside en route. He said okay, but I would need to fly to Indianapolis. I met him there and we drove to the base at Ft. Lee, VA.

Four weeks later in October, I asked Bill if he would consider driving to the Detroit area so I could drop off my valuable clarinet at home since I did not want to leave it on the base. Indiana, where he went to school, was playing Michigan State, where I graduated, in a football game at Spartan Stadium.

We only had a weekend to accomplish the ride to East Lansing and get back to the base at Ft. Lee, and we had a late start on a Friday.

I said to Bill, "we won't be able to make it and back in time, so we better stay here."

He responded saying that perhaps we can make a weekend out of it in Virginia and see some of the historic sites. Great idea. We shared a room at a motel in Richmond directly across the street from its Capitol. In the morning, we parked and left the motel only to see a large crowd on the grounds of the Capitol with American flags all over the place.

He said, let's go get breakfast and come back to the Capitol to see what was going on. As luck would have it, a half block from the Capitol near where we were staying, there was a diner with a sign that read "Massad and Deeb Restaurant." I said to Summers, what luck, I don't believe this. We walked to the diner and saw someone behind the counter, and asked him, "Is Mr. Deeb here?"

He responded "Yeah that's me, I'm Mr. Deeb." I responded, "Mr. Deeb, meet Mr. Deeb." He was so happy to see us, and asked where we were from. He thought we were there for the event at the Capitol.

We responded we are stationed at the Ft. Lee base, and we were headed to a football game in Michigan but we decided it was too far to make it in a weekend.

I had my expensive clarinet with me and wanted to take it back to Detroit.

"Hey guys, c'mon, sit down. Breakfast is on me," restaurant owner, Deeb said. He then asked us where we were from. Bill responded, Evansville, Indiana, and I said Detroit.

He responded, "I can't believe this, I'm originally from Detroit." He asked if I was born in Detroit. I said I was a native Detroiter.

He then informed us there was a big "hafli" or a Middle Eastern reception with music taking place after 6 p.m. at St. Anne's Church in Richmond. Perhaps you want to go. I'll call my pal Joe Yezbeck and let him know. He plays the derbeckee or Arabic drum.

We said to him we were going to meet some of the people across the street at the Capitol to see what was going on. We could meet Mr. Yezbeck around 6 p.m. and practice before heading to the club.

After meeting restaurataur Deeb and having a complimentary breakfast, we headed to the outdoor reception to learn what was going on. Several senators and other government people were in attendance.

We noted there was a young lady who looked frustrated. We asked if she was okay. She replied her public relations person had not arrived yet, and she wanted to get pictures of some of the important people here.

I responded my friend, Bill, here has a camera and can help by taking some photos and sending them to you. I have a communications degree and could help you prepare a brief news release if you want.

She got all excited and said, "If you guys would, I would deeply appreciate it." She then asked our names and where we were from. We told her.

She asked Bill to get some photos and asked me to follow her to their press room in the lobby of the hotel. She pointed to the typewriter on the desk and provided several sheets of paper. Bill kept asking, "what are you getting us into?"

I asked her who the group was and got the who, what, when and where etc and began drafting a news release for her.

It contained everything she wanted in it, and she made several copies to distribute to various media people attending.

She responded, "You guys really saved the day. Much appreciated."

Around 5 p.m., we called Mr. Yezbeck and said we would be able to meet him and practice our instruments – he with the derbekee, and me with the clarinet. After a half hour of practicing, he guided Bill and me to St. Anne's Church.

At the church, we were introduced as a couple of airmen who were stationed in Richmond. Ed plays the clarinet and will join me as I play the drum. But before the music and dancing, the ladies treated Bill and I to a tasty Middle Eastern meal, consisting of kibbe, tabbouleh, grape leaves and hummus. It was delicious.

We then began playing some music. Attendees were surprised that there was melody along with the drum. It was a memorable evening.

People asked us where we learned the Arabic music. I responded, "I learned it in Detroit and we carried it with us to East Lansing and MSU.

Following the "hafli" we went back to our barracks at the Base.

The next afternoon, we got a call from one of the co-chairman of the rally which took place at the Capitol. He stated the purpose of the event was to rally people to vote for either Nixon or Kennedy.

He said we saved the day for the committee by taking photos and writing the press release which was sent to the local media. He said if we had time late afternoons after duty, they would love us to assist them at the Capitol.

We said we would for about two weeks, after hours. A day later, they called to say they were picking up Bobby Kennedy at the airport. Would we like to go? We said we would be happy to. We did.

All the time we left the Base in the late afternoon, our colleagues at the base kept asking us where are you going? We told them to volunteer our time for the elections. They never believed us.

The night of the election, a large reception was held at the Richmond hotel. Prominent people were everywhere, along with plenty of food and photographers.

Bill and I realized a couple of the photographers took photos of us, but we did not give it a second thought.

Then, early the next morning, we arrived on Base and headed for our bunks ... when all of a sudden the lights went on and our colleagues were up asking us about the reception.

We asked, "how did you find out about it?" They said, "Your picture was in the newspaper. On our bunks, the picture page of the local paper was on our beds with our photos in it.

A once in a lifetime experience!

FIRST JOB JITTERS

AFTER MY ACTIVE duty tenure in the U.S. Air Force and the Reserves, I needed to find a job in my career field. My major was communication arts and sciences with an emphasis on journalism and communications.

This is my first effort to find a job following my years in college and the Air Force. What do I do? Where do I go?

Someone said to me, go to the Adcraft Club in Detroit which meets monthly where many people in advertising, journalism, communication etc. attend. The same person told me, "See if you can meet with the current president, Toby David." Toby was with CKLW radio and TV. "He may know of some company that might have some work at the office that they can give you or some company that has an opening."

So, I attended the luncheon and met several of the people who were members of the Club including the president, Mr.

David. At the end of the luncheon, I had a chance to talk to Toby and told him I graduated college recently and just completed a tour of duty in the Air Force, and I am looking for a job in the communications field.

He said, "I think there is an opening with a publishing firm which publishes four different food industry newspapers including the Grocers Spotlight Newspaper, and they are looking for somebody to fill one of the positions. They were located on Woodward Avenue in the Fox Building.

When I got to the office of the publishing company, they introduced me to the founder and current president Louis Shamie. He said, "We do have an opening but it is to coordinate the pages for printing the stories. Do you have any knowledge in that area?" I said, "I would like to be a writer, but since this is my first real job following college, I would be happy to start at the bottom and move up." He said, "I have the opening presently and you can start the job next Monday, if you are interested." I said I was and I would be there to start my first job.

The job was really reading story copy for any errors and helping them to lay out the pages. It was not a difficult job, but I thought it would give me a chance to move up the ladder.

Then, unexpectedly, two months later, the editor of the publishing company resigned to take a job at another publishing company. The president and board members were nervous that they had to do all the papers without somebody assisting them as a writer. When I heard about it, I said to Mr. Shamie, "you know I would be happy to write these stories for you since that was my major." He said, "I am going to put something in front of you and see how you handle it."

So he put some information in front of me, some easy, some medium and some hard, and I wrote the stories. He said, "This is terrific. This is exactly what we need. We are promoting you to writer and news editor."

I began following up on leads and stories and writing them and meeting several prominent people in the food distribution industry and attending their events.

5

THE BUSINESS
ASSOCIATION

AFTER TWO YEARS, (in 1962), I was called by the president
of the Food Dealers of Detroit for a meeting. I thought it was
for a story on their organization. Instead, he said the group's
executive was retiring and because of my experience with the
food industry newspaper he wanted to discuss hiring me as
director, editor, and CEO.

He indicated the organization had not been growing and
it was losing members. After a couple of days, I indicated I
would take the job, and notified the newspaper that I would
be leaving in two weeks.

At my first meeting with the board members, I learned
they did not have any programs going, only monthly board
meetings. So I began talking with various grocers and

community leaders and learned what was needed to get the food association more active and growing.

Among the things I learned and launched for the group involved the following:

- A workshop between retailers and suppliers to improve ways to deal with problems.
- Since many stores were being robbed at the time, we launched a program where suppliers picked a day to circle the location areas indicating where crimes could be reduced.
- I launched a program called AVOW. (Alert Vendors on Watch) to help curb problems near their businesses.
- I next began an awards program to recognize individuals in the industry, to include a grocer, supplier, broker, community leader, elected official and a media person. It became quite popular and the dinner was well attended.
- I met with government officials to discuss problems which needed to be corrected or resolved.I launched several insurance programs, as life, disability, health and others, with Blue Cross and Blue Shield. This turned out to be probably the most popular.
- In addition, I professionalized the group's newsletter and magazine to provide suggestions for customer relations and business improvement.

During my 20 year tenure, the organization grew from 92 members to 4,000 members.

There were several important projects we had to get involved in. The first was the move by environmentalists to charge a deposit fee on soft drinks and beer containers. It was felt by them that this would clean up the communities.

As an industry organization, we opposed the effort, simply because it would add huge expenses to store owners, taverns, and restaurants, most which were small businesses.

The official industry position arguing against the need for additional beverage can and bottle deposits were Peter Stroh of Stroh Brewery Co., Mort Feigenson of Faygo Beverages, a soft drink company, and myself representing retailers, restaurants, and taverns. We ran a strong campaign, but we lost in the elections, and thus started returnable beverage containers which now had a 10 cent monetary deposits on them.

I did not have a job when I left my previous organization, so I decided to form the Michigan Food and Beverage Association to become liaison to assist retailers in the trade, and the Michigan Business and Professional Association to assist businesses outside the food industry.

Some of the board members of my old association thought I was trying to compete with them. That really never crossed my mind. The reason I began MFBA and later MBPA was because they were statewide organizations, not simply Detroit area based.

What do you do when you start a new business? You let people know about it. So I called a news conference and invited representatives from all local media.

The effort to do so involved more work than I thought of, because it was a new organization. To begin with, I needed a board of directors, begin a newsletter, and monthly magazine, and launch several programs to assist those who needed help.

The next day, I started getting calls from those interested in assisting me or serving on an advisory board, deciding the goals and programs of the new MFBA.

I began by forming a small board, people who were familiar with the food industry and supermarkets. The list included Louis Vescio, Phil Lauri, Don Harrington, and myself in the beginning.

We began publishing a bi-weekly newsletter and a bi-monthly magazine called the Associations Spotlight. Because of my journalism background, we were able to write the stories and publish in about a week or twice a month.

By the end of the first year, we were able to sign up 1,100 new members. We grew to 5,500 members in four years.

6

RIOTING IS NOT
THE ANSWER

REGARDING THE **1967** rioting in Detroit, I kept records of some 400 incidents where retail stores were either vandalized, affected by fire, theft of merchandise, etc. Retailers called to say their stores were being looted or burned.

My compilation of information as president of Michigan Food and Beverage Association at that time (1967), involving the rioting and the 400 incidents involving food stores was so valuable to the U.S. Senate Subcommittee in Washington that they petitioned me to bring a copy of this report to the capitol and testify before the committee. I followed those who testified before I did, namely Michigan Gov. George Romney, Detroit Mayor Jerome Cavanaugh and the Detroit police chief.

Later the group from the U.S. Senate Committee came to Detroit to gather information on the rioting to learn if there was anything positive that could be learned or reported. At the start of the rioting, I began learning as to how much damage was done to each food store, supermarket or convenience store ... whether slightly damaged like broken windows, or totally destroyed by fire. It was a frustrating time for store owners, many who stood atop their stores to help protect their property.

We must keep in mind there is not just one type of ethnicity in Detroit. Like most large cities, there were many ethnic groups, as Irish, Italian, African American, Middle Eastern, Polish, German and Russian to name a few.

With numerous problems in a community, an exodus began. It was inevitable that larger food stores, for example, as Great Scott, Farmer Jack, A&P, Chatham and others would stop operating in a city which lacked harmony, tranquility, or protection.

Detroit was lucky that when several of the larger supermarkets which left the city at the time, after the rioting, several entrepreneurs and employees of larger independent markets began taking over the closed stores simply to be able to keep the food supply going.

As head of the Michigan Food and Beverage Association at the time, calls were coming in to me complaining about the rioting and destruction taking place.

During this terrible time, I kept wondering what needed to be done. I formed an organization with Walter Douglas of New Detroit, Frances Kornegay, head of the Detroit Urban League, NAACP, and attorney Salman Sesi of the Arabic-Chaldean American community to respond to questions which came in. We urged residents and business people to be more sensitive and try to get the city calmed down and back to normal. Fr. William Cunningham of Focus:Hope also played a key role. Our committee began meeting with citizens and retailers to begin solving problems in the area.

Also, Detroit area grocers of Middle Eastern background (Arabic and Chaldean-Iraqi, Syrian and Lebanese) began reopening their stores, or purchasing larger stores which were closed. This was one of the positives which occurred.

We urged merchants to support local charities, schools and churches; to hold an annual picnic for their customers in their store parking lot; to hire local people where possible; and show that store owners truly wanted to be respected and part of the community.

With improved regular communications, much harmony began to focus. NDI and MFBA focused on relationships to help keep peace and tranquility in the area.

I started to be called the "chief trouble shooter and peacemaker" in the community and food industry. Each day we had different issues involving store owners. The key to bringing peace and tranquility between the parties was to have dialogue; and to have the conflicting parties meet to discuss the various issues. This worked out quite well.

When it comes to major problems or minor situations, a business must be able to deal with them and offer solutions, and find answers to show customers you care about them.

CESAR CHAVEZ AND THE GRAPE BOYCOTT

Another type of issue we personally helped resolve, involved the matter of a grape boycott staged by Cesar

Chavez of the Grape Growers Union from California. Several representatives of the Grape Growers organization began picketing food stores in Detroit. I received numerous calls. I decided to go meet with some of the growers. I got information on such boycotts. I later went into the area where picketers were, and surprisingly, met with Cesar Chavez himself picketing.

I said to Mr. Chavez, "Are you aware that you and your people cannot picket food stores in this manner?" He said, 'why not?" I said, "because this represents a secondary boycott and you and your team could be arrested and spend time in jail." "No, I did not know that", he replied. So he called his people and left Detroit immediately.

I have given several examples about what happens or could happen if regular communications between residents and store owners take place. It is the best way to deal with problems or misunderstandings. As I said, rioting is not the answer.

Recently, I celebrated 60 years as an association leader. I recall in the beginning, I established a hotline to call and learn of complaints or incidents taking place involving merchants. It was also a time when crimes such as robberies and burglaries against store owners were higher than ever, and some merchants were shot and killed in their stores.

Finally following the rioting, better race relations and diversity began showing up and taking place.

7

WE'RE ALL IN THIS TOGETHER

DETROIT, TODAY, IS in a strong comeback! For years, the city was losing population and jobs. Individuals who came from ethnic groups began working closer with other ethnic groups. Individual cultures began reaching across the fence, doing more things together regardless of their ethnicity. Organizations and groups throughout the city became more diverse.

In one dictionary, "diversity" is defined as "differing from one another; inclusion of different cultures and relating to diverse cultures."

Today, such things as trends and topics, being together, living together, working together is commonplace. In this regard, the issues like healthcare, our aging communities, workforce, and multi-culturism are often formally discussed.

The topic of diversity and the "melting pot" concept worked well before; they should be able to work even better today. Our goal should also be to assist people not only to achieve the American Dream, but also build better communities, cities, states, and nation.

And, by working closer together through diversity, we will be able to strive for better schools, reduce crime on the streets, achieve greater results in education for our kids, be more productive, and be more harmonious people. This is how our community succeeds.

But saying this is easy. The difficulty is to begin. Most of us have lived thinking, "the American Dream" will come soon. But to do so, we must work for it.

Key question: What are we waiting for? Let's start today.

Later, in 2020, we experienced something even more important –something that not only "coronavirus pandemic" that affected not only the U.S. but most every nation on earth. Several thousands of individuals from all over the world died as a result before it ended.

You had to give credit to President Trump, his national leaders and medical staff, the major corporations throughout the world which were affected, as China, Italy, our several U.S. states, and other nations, along with our Senators, House members, the numerous large corporations who helped solve the problem, small corporations, food companies, religious leaders and so many universities etc. for, yes, coming together to solve the coronavirus threat despite any differences.

Kudos went to the doctors, nurses, health care people, and first responders who played an important role in helping defeat the virus.

Personally, I have not seen so much cooperation in our nation and the world since I learned how the world came together during World War II.

This is the kind of cooperation we need all the time to prevent problems and keep our nation and the world more united.

YOUTH APPRECIATION EXPERIENCE

IN **PART OF** running a business or charitable organization, we found it is important that we support the volunteers, and be good citizens in the community. This is a must.

After the altercations occurred on Livernois and the rioting in Detroit, we decided we had to get involved to help solve problems in the community-at-large. I decided something had to be done to "inspire our youth to do the most good." I formed Michigan Youth Appreciation Foundation and Metro Detroit Youth Day to let the youth and community leaders know we cared about them and wanted solutions. Some of the problems were looting, destruction at retail shops in Detroit by youngsters.

I was in touch with Mayor Coleman Young, some City Council people, and some media people. We eventually worked with a coalition to concentrate on better relationships in the community. All of us wanted to inspire their youth to be our future leaders in Detroit, and Michigan and even nationally too.

START OF YOUTH DAY

After we formed the Michigan Youth Appreciation Foundation, in 1980, I got a call from Tom Fox of WJBK-TV and Jerry Blocker of WWJ radio who wanted to help out. I mentioned to them we were thinking of something to get school kids and youngsters to concentrate on more important things than stealing items from retail stores. The questions became: Where do we start? Let's meet first with area grocers who were upset and wanted something done.

Fox, Jerry and I were invited to the TV2 studios to discuss how we can get young people involved in an annual event featuring various interesting things to do, like various games (football, basketball, soccer, tennis, song and dance contests, etc.) But where do we hold such an event?

It was decided to invite representatives from 25 youth organizations and run the idea by them. We asked the group, "Would you be willing to send your group to an event that could have a variety of things to do, and a free lunch at noon?"

All those in attendance raised their hands to state they would like that. So, we had to decide where would this event be held, and what would we offer the youngsters so as to enjoy it?

Being I grew up on the eastside near Eastern High, six blocks north of the Belle Isle Bridge, I suggested Belle Isle's

Athletic Field. I suggested this site since it was not being used by anyone or any group at the time.

Metro Detroit Youth Day as part of the Michigan Youth Appreciation Foundation, a non-profit organization, was the name we selected so all the youngsters from the tri-county area of Detroit would be able to attend. So we had to decide what do we include in this event, and how do we serve a breakfast and lunch?

We met with officials of the City of Detroit and those of the Detroit Recreation Department. They finally concluded that since the Athletic Field at Belle Isle was not being used, they felt it would be ideal for Metro Detroit Youth Day and the program we had outlined.

It was then decided to call Mayor Young to ask if he would host our first meeting with the 25 organizations. He agreed, and more than 35 organizations showed up. With the Mayor's urging and our follow up, we began plans to host the first meeting at Belle Isle's Athletic Field, unused at the time.

The groups also included YMCA, The Salvation Army, Boys & Girls Clubs, Boys & Girls Scouts, Urban League, the Arabic schools, etc. to name a few.

When we set out to plan all the items needed for such a program outdoors without tables and chairs, nor a stage with a microphone, we knew it would take a lot of work, volunteers and funding from concerned business corporations to get the job done.

After much activity and promotions our set-up, included arranging for a free lunch, we had a late start and so only had 1,200 youngsters who attended the first event. But, it was successful and all parties and chaperones said they looked forward to next year (1982). A huge thanks goes out to the various food vendors, suppliers, and food industry companies for the lunches they provided. They are great supporters.

Even due to the smaller turnout, we began getting numerous calls asking why they did not get invited or phoned. We said we would add them to the roster for 1982.

We also got phone calls and letters stating the parents wanted to be involved the following year. And so this colorful event grew regularly each year and in 2018, our 36th year, we drew 38,000 youngsters from the tri-county area schools, and even youngsters from other parts of Michigan and Ontario, Canada.

In 2019, we expected more than 35,000 youngsters, greeted by a breakfast when they arrive at the Athletic Field, 51 different activities from which the kids could choose to participate in including tutoring from the Lions, Pistons and Tigers players, along with a tasty lunch, entertainment on stage, 16 colleges and universities who participated, and it keeps growing.

We also began honoring those individuals who gave of their time to help the kids. Individuals like star athletes Lem Barney, Lomas Brown, Willie Horton, Dave Bing, Joe Dumars, Bob Probert, "Night train" Lane, Ted Lindsay, Bill Lambeer, Isaiah Thomas, Jalen Rose, Ron Rice, and Vinnie Johnson to name a few who attended to coach the kids.

Also visiting us through the years involved Mayor Coleman Young, his son Sen. Colman Young II, Martha Reeves, Gov. Jennifer Granholm, Gov. Jim Blanchard, Gov. Gretchen Whitmer, Gov. George Romney, Gov. Bill Milliken, John

Conti, Robert Ficano, Ice Cube and Dave Bing to mention some who attended to join us and inspired the kids.

We also began giving out college scholarships. By 2018 we gave out more than 2,000 of them. We also average more than 1,500 volunteers each year, and received numerous awards. Recognitions included the Point of Light Award from President George H.W. Bush, Shining Light Award from the Detroit Free Press, the Governor's Council on Physical Fitness, and awards from The Detroit News, and various counties and individuals to mention a few.

Michigan Youth Appreciation Foundation became incorporated by a committee of Youth Day founders. Foundations are included and are tax exempt. Without the more than 250 corporate sponsors, we would not be able to put on the highly successful Youth Day event.

Among the initial organizations who were supporting this effort included, Ford Motor Company Fund, United Way, Comerica Bank, Chase Bank, The Skillman Foundation, General Motors, Volkswagen, FCA Chrysler, Focus:Hope, T-Mobile, Wolverine Packing, The Salvation Army, New Detroit, AT&T and many others.

This is not an event we should only do in Detroit, but the entire national community should strive for all of us being better. Remember our youth are our future leaders. Help us "inspire them to do the most good."

The more active an individual is from various organizations, the more success one can achieve.

THANKS FOR THE PROBLEM SOLVERS

I **LEARNED THROUGH** experience there are a variety of problems which may occur in running a business. The owner or management must be able to resolve their problems in a timely and respectful manner. You must quickly learn running a business is not easy.

In the association management business you need to learn many skills as writing, directing, promoting, advertising in newspapers, magazines, radio, and television, I learned that there are many different types of problem solvers, and problem solving. Many individuals who start a business do <u>not</u> even have an outline of goals, or outcomes to keep track of sales and profits.

While many individuals are able to generally operate a business without a structure or goals, in order to assure success along with record-keeping, you must develop an outline or method for solving unforeseen problems.

I found that problems which need attention, and problem solving take many different forms whether in running a business or helping to solve problems in your community or industry.

Running a retail store, of course, you need to assure you have a variety of products or services competitively prices to help assure growth.

Community problems can mean dealing with an angry customer, a dissatisfied committee, a neighborhood or nearby church. Problems come in many forms. For example:

Food - Problems you may need to deal with are spoiled products, fresh produce, canned goods, frozen foods, non-frozen foods, etc.

Knowing the Laws - In Michigan, in 1976 a beverage container law was passed supported by the consuming public. It meant placing a 10 cent deposit on all beverage containers. This created numerous problems for retailers (many who vaguely understood English) to create or expand to have more room in stores, charge the customers the fee (and at the beginning were not accustomed to paying an extra dime or nickel.)

Crimes - There are different types of crimes committed at retail stores, which increase the cost of doing business. Such as returning non-returnable soda bottles and cans which were not marked for the 10 cent deposit. A regular loss of money.

Robberies - Product theft, and other types of crime confronting retailers regularly.

<u>Recordkeeping</u> of employees, paying bills, taxes, accounting, promotions, etc. to name a few areas. One must keep records, pay appropriate taxes, and file an annual income tax sent by the IRS.

Also, product prices should be competitive and products should be fresh and the best available always.

<u>Some Examples</u>

Arguments may arise from an issue for not charging the correct price, or selling alcoholic beverages to minors, or being affected by area altercations or rioting.`

When it comes to major problems or minor situations, a business must be able to deal with them and offer solutions, and find answers to show customers you care about them.

I have given several examples about what happens or could happen if someone did not properly run their business.

As an association executive, I learned there are a variety of problems which may occur in running a business. The owner or management must be able to resolve their problems in a timely and respectful manner. It is not easy.

Thus when managing an association or company, you need to be able to deal with several areas. As president or top executive, you deal with members, boards of directors, event chairpersons, financial people, etc., just to mention a few. The more smoothly an organization is managed, the fewer problems you will encounter.

As I mentioned earlier about the Detroit rioting in 1967, some major problems cannot be solved by one person alone. Solving involves putting together a team from major organizations including governmental agencies to obtain a solution.

You need to create and help direct others in your mission for peace. You would be smart to get those who dealt with major problems if possible, trouble shooters and peacemakers would help. They would help define where the problems lie, and direct individuals as peacemakers who would meet personally with those creating problems, as in the rioting mentioned and assisting with other problems as the grape boycott as mentioned earlier.

There Ought to be a Law
Against Killing Time

Mort Crim
Television Anchor

Time is the great equalizer.

Everybody starts the day with the same 24 hours staring them in the face.

It doesn't matter how rich you are or how poor. Whether you work in an office or a factory or don't work at all. Time plays no favorites with people or positions.

Success in life depends heavily upon how well we learn to use this most valuable, nonrenewable resource. Once it's gone, whether invested wisely or squandered foolishly, it can never be recaptured.

That's why, in my view, killing time should be a capital offense. Just think what can be – and is – accomplished by people who've learned to utilize that odd moment, to collect and exploit an extra hour here and there. People have earned college degrees and pilot's licenses, written books and started businesses simply by taking advantage of spare time.

It wasn't that they had any more time than the next person. They may not necessarily have been brighter or more talented. They simply recognized what can be done when time is respected and invested.

What is it in your life that you *think* you don't have time for?

Would you like to learn computers? Become a beautician? A photographer? Improve your parenting skills? Become an accountant? I've seen the power of pulling together wasted minutes and hours. There's plenty of evidence that we can do just about anything we want to do in our spare time.

That is, once we stop *killing* it.

– Mort Crim
"Second Thoughts"

10

MOVING UP THE LADDER

WHEN YOU ARE new in your job, you not only think of how you can help your employer, but along the way, you meet interesting people who work for different companies and, especially when you are from a professional or trade association.

These individuals are regularly looking for people they feel can help their company improve, excel or grow. The same is true when you start a new organization as we did to help solve a community problem following the rioting of 1967, creating Metro Detroit Youth Day, and its umbrella organization, Michigan Youth Appreciation Foundation.

Then when you have a way of helping solve problems, the area news media want to know about how it was done and who are the people who did it.

Thus over the years, people get to know you and the talent or experiences you have. As a result, one example was from Michigan State University. I graduated from the then newly formed College of Communication Arts (and later it added – and Sciences). It was the newest program added to MSU in 1955.

I happened to be one of the first 45 persons to major in this College. My area was journalism and advertising. Comm Arts as it was called, was located in the oldest building left on campus at the time. Students wondered (1) When are we going to get a new building? Our classes were in a farm house, the last oldest buildings on the main campus.

And, (2) When were we going to establish the College of Communication Arts and Sciences Alumni Association so as to hold events in the name of this area.

Since we did not have such an alumni organization after we graduated, we printed a list of all 45 graduates, and occasionally met for lunch or dinner to see how we were all doing, and whether we heard of any job openings. (Today, we have more than 5,000 alumni in the College of Communication Arts alone.)

After a couple of years went by, I got a call from the Dean of Comm Arts, who said they would like to see me on campus. The following week I went to East Lansing and met with Dr Jack Bain and Jack Breslin.

They indicated to me they would like to start an alumni association, and they wanted me to head it. (At the time I was managing the area food and beverage association.) Obviously, I was thrilled to learn of this and asked how do you want to set it up? They replied, first you had to create a board of directors, and then establish by-laws for the organization.

They left the choosing of board members up to me since I knew most of the grads in my 1960 class. We wanted to include all categories taught in the college, as journalism, advertising, radio and television, theater, etc.

We then called a meeting to review the contents of the by-laws of the Comm Arts group, and recommended 14 board members, representing all the various Comm Arts courses taught in the college. Since it was a voluntary organization, it took about a year and a half to finalize the by-laws and took five meetings to do so.

The very first event was at an informal breakfast held at MSU's Kellogg Center, to honor a male and female graduate from our college, and present our first awards the morning of an MSU football game. We would be able to watch the game afterward.

From then on the various programs, activities, award dinners, etc, grew over the years. Today, I am happy to report as the first president of the MSU College of Communication Arts & Sciences, the total enrollment today in this college is around 4,500 students annually.

For my efforts in getting the alumni organization started, and involved in creating several events, the college surprised me by naming a room in the building after me, and presenting me with a Distinguished Alumni Award.

A couple of years later, I got a call from MSU Vice-President, Jack Breslin. He invited me to an event on campus and gave me the location. When I arrived, I saw a large outdoor tent on a field of grass, and a line of silver shovels. Breslin saw me and waved me over to him. He said, "In case you haven't figured this out, it is the groundbreaking of the new Communication Arts Building, and for all you have done for MSU's College of Communication Arts and Sciences and being the founder of the alumni organization, we wanted you to join us and dig with a shovel."

11

HONORING WOMEN WHO THRIVE

AFTER **20** YEARS as the leader and expander of the Detroit area food and beverage dealers association, I left the organization to start the Michigan Food and Beverage Association and the Michigan Business and Professional Association, both statewide organizations.

Some of the board members of my old association thought I was trying to compete with them. That really never crossed my mind. The reason I began MFBA and later MBPA was because they were statewide organizations, not simply Detroit area based. We started a health care program with Blue Cross Blue Shield of Michigan.

The effort to do so involved more work than I thought of, because it was a new organization. To begin with, I needed to form a board of directors, begin a newsletter, and monthly magazine, and launch several programs to assist those who needed help.

I began by forming a small board, people who were familiar with the food industry and supermarkets. The list included Louis Vescio, Phil Lauri, Don Harrington, and myself at the beginning.

We began publishing a bi-weekly newsletter and a bi-monthly magazine called the Associations Spotlight. Because of my journalism background, we were able to write the stories and publish in about a week or twice a month.

How could we compete with more established organizations? As a non-profit organization, we started a coupon redemption service, we worked with insurance agents to start a health insurance program (Blue Cross), a life insurance program, inaugurated several programs to attract retailers and suppliers, held several workshops and an exposition. This helped us grow faster.

We began inviting various government leaders – representatives and senators to speak at our events. All the government people enjoyed the outdoor reception and picnic we held in front of the State Capitol. We did this for several years.

As an organization, we began getting invitations to speak at various events and programs ourselves.

At one of our board meetings one of the women asked, "Why do you not have events for women? You could have a specific agenda for speakers, then a luncheon to follow. At the luncheon, you could begin honoring women leaders in Michigan." We thought it was a great idea, and started the women's program with awards a couple of months later.

In conjunction with the women's program, we appointed a board of women leaders who helped establish the agendas for our meetings and created a list of potential women honorees. It was called "Women and Leadership in the Workplace."

Vernice Davis Anthony, St. John/Ascension Health; Elaine Baker, Oldies 104.3 WOMC; Eleanor Josaitis, Focus:Hope; Grace Gilchrist, WXYZ-TV7; Betty Jean Awrey, Awrey Bakeries; Helen Love, Ford Motor Company; Lou Anna Simon, Michigan State University; Geneva Williams, United Way Community Services; Maryann Mahaffey, Detroit City Council; Irma Elder, Elder Ford; Hon. Dorothy Comstock Riley, Michigan Supreme Court; Roberta Jasina, WWJ Newsradio 950, Patricia Cole, Cole Financial Services to name a few.

This program is still going strong and chaired by my daughter, Jennifer Kluge who re-named it "Women Who Thrive Awards." It is a fantastic program. During the first ten years we honored more than 100 women.

HONOREES FROM WOMEN IN LEADERSHIP CONFERENCES

Irma Elder
Elder Ford

Dr. Jane Thomas
Wayne State Univ

Hon. Dorothy
Comstock-Riley
Michigan
Supreme Court

Maggie Allesse
Humanitarian

Dr. Glenda Price
Marygrove University

Monica Gayle
Fox 2 WJBK

Roberta Jasina
WWJ Newsradio 950

Lou Anna Simon
Michigan State Univ.

Jennifer Kluge
MI Business &
Professional Assn

SURVIVAL OF DETROIT'S EASTERN MARKET

WE **ALMOST LOST** historic Eastern Market, the city's popular farmers market when vendors and merchants almost left. Many of the regular patrons of Detroit's historic farmers market called Eastern Market were not aware that at one time there was the possibility that it almost closed, ending a tradition of having the farmers and retailers sell their fruits, vegetables, meats and flowers.

But thanks to the forward thinking of several key individuals, we formed the Eastern Market Corporation in 2008 and urged the City to permit the people at the Market to run Eastern Market because of their vast knowledge of food, the vendors, and since the area itself is one of the largest farmers markets in the U.S. along with Faneuil Hall in Boston and Pike's Market in Seattle. Following is the history of Eastern Market from the beginning.

Detroit's Farmer's Market is celebrating its 213th birthday in 2020. The first 39 years it was located at the foot of Woodward at the Detroit River, before moving to Cadillac Square in 1841. Then at its present site in 1891 the Farmer's Market was re-named Eastern Market and has been at its current location for 125+ years.

From the horse-drawn carts to the present semi-trailer trucks, farmers have annually hauled thousands of tons of fresh produce to Detroit's Eastern Market area for re-sale to wholesalers, retailers and the general public. The figure is estimated to be nearly 100,000 tons per year.

Today, on any given Saturday, some 50,000 Detroiters, suburbanites, and out-of-staters at Eastern Market can be found shopping elbow-to-elbow at farmers stalls or area retail shops for products from as near as Michigan, Ohio and Canadian farms or as far away as the Europe, Middle East, Asia and South America farming areas.

Historic Eastern Market area is not only known for its luscious, colorful farm fresh fruits and vegetables, but also for its meat and fish products, the herbs and spices, nuts, candies, and a variety of condiments supplied by retailers and wholesalers.

Most people are unaware most of the businesses are open six days a week. The public farmers market in the sheds are open mainly on Saturdays, and on special days in the summer months. An annual Flower Day is held at Eastern Market each year, offering bedding plants, flowers, shrubs, evergreens, etc. It is recognized as the world's largest bedding flower market, held in May, the Sunday after Mother's Day. Eastern Market Merchants Assn. (EMMA) was asked by the Flower Growers Association to assist them in promoting the annual colorful Flower Day event, since their shoppers were dwindling. EMMA added several new items and other products to enhance customer choices and attendance at the flower event.

Eastern Market means "family", as several generations have shopped together, bringing their children to see the market, its wares and the farm animals when available. It is also a people watcher's delight. Rich and poor, old and young, browse and actually bargain old-world style for what suits their interests, absorbing the sights and sounds, color and excitement of the Eastern Market area.

Many couples and families make an "outing" out of shopping here, arriving before 7 a.m. having breakfast at one of the area's restaurants, then spending the morning shopping for their weekly needs.

Although an open-air farmers' market existed prior to the Civil War, the first sales shed was built in 1891 in the Vernor, Russell, Gratiot Avenues amid several other food establishments which had already located in the area. As the market area prospered, additional sheds were constructed in 1922 and 1929. Through the post-Depression era, Eastern Market area grew, expanding in size.

In the Fall, Ford Field, home of the Detroit Lions, was about to open nearby. Frustrated Ford Field officials called me and said they were unable to hold tailgate parties on the streets. Eastern Market Merchants Association and Michigan Food and Beverage Association was asked to work out an arrangement with them so Lions fans can park and tailgate at

Eastern Market in designated areas. So, I arranged a meeting with City officials to approve tailgating at the nearby Market for the Detroit Lions, provided they would clean the streets the day after each home game, and be responsible for the snow removal in the area during winter months.

Four Historic Events Took Place that helped shape Eastern Market to the present day. THE FIRST was the end of World War II when our servicemen victoriously came home, settled down, getting married and having a family. At the same time, pre-packaged foods and the beginning of the modern supermarkets, shoppers changed the way they shopped, being able to get food products in one store.

THE SECOND was when EMMA and various businesses at Eastern Market decided they needed to create events and other activities to draw the people back to the Eastern Market. Since I was president of the State's largest food industry association, I was personally contacted by the Eastern Market merchants to create a new association to help draw people back to the Market and better communicate with government officials.

Thus Eastern Market Merchants Association (EMMA) was formed in 1972. Officers were Ed Deeb, founder and chairman and Sal Ciaramitaro was elected president. EMMA board members included Jim Vitale, Gerry Fermanis, John Vivio, Tim McCarthy, and Tom DeVries, Sr. Eastern Market became an important hub for the southeastern Michigan food distribution industry.

EMMA began planning parades down Russell Street with the Shriners and Knights of Columbus. They also invited Gospel singers to the Market to put on concerts, and even had a Gospelfest contest with several churches. They also planned special product promotions and had several cooking classes in Shed 5 at the Market with special community events. And began the annual "Blessing of the Harvest" event each Fall. The annual Flower Day event was launched as well.

THE THIRD historic event was when the association and several members appealed to City officials to allow them to form a non-profit corporation to operate Eastern Market themselves. After several meetings in the City, they agreed to give the new Eastern Market Corporation (EMC) authority to operate the Market to demonstrate they were able to improve Eastern Market area professionally. Crowds and shoppers were much larger than ever.

At the same time in 2006 the new Eastern Market Corporation was formed. (Founders of the Eastern Market Corporation were Walt Watkins, Ed Deeb, George Jackson and Kate Beebe.) They hired Dan Carmody who came to Detroit from Ft. Wayne, Indiana. He was thrilled to be the new manager in Detroit, a bigger city.

His prior market was much smaller, in Ft. Wayne, Indiana.

As a result, several companies, community organizations, and foundations began channeling needed finances to the Eastern Market through the new Corporation and allowing it to renovate sheds and spruce up the Market. This was well received by the community, farmers, and vendors. Thus more people come to the Market today than ever before. Historic Eastern Market developed into an important hub for the southeastern Michigan food distribution industry. Plans are to make it bigger, better and more efficient for the future.

Since the non-profit EMC was formed in 2006, several millions of dollars were donated to improve the Market area. Various foundation indicated they preferred to donate to a 501-c-3 corporation directly rather than a government agency (city).

Eastern Market was originally declared an historic area in 1977 by the State of Michigan Historical Commission. Many of the original buildings are still in operation or standing today.

THE HISTORIC POINTS OF INTEREST INCLUDE:

- Sacred Heart Church
- Roma Café, renamed Amore de Roma
- R. Hirt, Jr. Co., renamed DeVries & Co. 1887
- Ciaramitaro Bros. Produce building,
- Vivio's Restaurant
- Butchers Saloon Building
- Cost Plus Wine Shop
- Gratiot Central Market, on Gratiot Ave, Building is owned by the Bedway Family

THE FOURTH interesting phase began in 2008 when Shed 2 was completely renovated. Shortly thereafter Shed 3 was completely renovated and used also to hold events and activity.

In 2015, Shed 5 was transformed into a State of the Art facility. It holds cooking classes, food festivals, and a community kitchen, and gathering place for lunch, among other amenities.

Other interesting tidbits include the fact that Generals Ulysses S. Grant, George Custer, and John J. Pershing were headquartered in the area and marched troops up and down the area where the Eastern Market is presently located.

In addition, parts of the Underground Railroad went from the Eastern Market to the Detroit River where escaping slaves were able to make safe haven to Canada through an underground tunnel beneath the old Ciaramitaro building. Also, part of an ancient American Indian burial ground was located in the area, and later relocated to a nearby cemetery.

The historic Eastern Market area is the site of a summer full of special events throughout the year. In 2011 the Market began opening a successful Tuesday Market with farmers (June-Sept., in addition to Saturday's all-day Market. Also, a Sunday Street Market is open (June-Sept.).

Several movies were filmed at Eastern Market, including "Presumed Innocent" starring Harrison Ford and Brian Dennehy and "Collision Course" with Jay Leno and Pat Morita.

Newly renovated Shed 3 and Shed 5 today can accommodate large parties, receptions, workshops, seminars, etc. It's more interesting than ever.

Today, the market area is expanding with more and various shops and services, a larger Market staff, and an active boards of directors. The Market today is flourishing with various events, banquets, additional vendors and greater activity. Eastern Market is considered one of the largest farmers markets nationally.

(For information on historic Eastern Market, feel free to contact the writer, Ed Deeb, phone (586) 774-4000 or (313) 605-5700 (cell)

History written by Ed Deeb, Founder and Chairman
Founder, Eastern Market Merchants Assn.
Founder, Friends of Eastern Market
Co-Founder, Eastern Market Corporation, and
Founder, Michigan Food and Beverage Association
26333 E. Jefferson, Suite 101
St. Claire Shores, MI 48081

13

THE PEACEMAKERS AND TROUBLESHOOTERS

FOLLOWING ALL OF the incidents and discussions, we began holding monthly workshops with fellow students and faculty on how to deal with various customers and future programs as well as conflicting situations.

We also started a speakers bureau where several of our organizations would also feature speakers at schools, parent groups, and various workshops etc.

All of this helped to restore the peace, tranquility, and confidence in our communities and country following the rioting of 1967 and currently as well.

At the same time, we encouraged smaller retailers and food store operators to start taking over the larger food chain units that had left the city, such as Farmer Jack, A&P, Great Scott, National and others. This helped restore confidence with communities and providing confidence for shoppers knowing there was more variety stores coming back to the city to choose from.

Wherever a problem ensued between a retailer and people in a community, we sent out troubleshooters to help calm the area and restore the peace. This turned out to be a key element in restoring peaceful relations and confidence in the various neighborhoods around Detroit.

Today, the comeback made in the City of Detroit and Southeast Michigan has been phenomenal. Large corporations, more stores, restaurants, larger farmers markets, and fast food restaurants, to name some of the areas which are thriving today.

Of course you need to thank our politicians, too, such as Governors William Milliken, George Romney, John Engler and Mayors such as Dave Bing, Dennis Archer, Coleman A. Young and Mike Duggan who lent helping hands when needed.

THANKS TO THOSE WHO
LENT A HELPING HAND

In writing this book, it meant trying to remember those persons who worked with me, or at a major project as our annual Metro Detroit Youth Day and our Michigan Youth Appreciation Foundation, they were very important projects to help our kids and keep them away from problems.

It was at MSU where I learned of the importance of being positive and building a positive program. I learned what important roles of journalism, public relations, media, radio, and television play in various committees, in our societies, and our nation as well.

My first lesson was when I auditioned and received a four-year scholarship from MSU's Leonard Falcone to attend the university, playing clarinet in the marching band, and later in the concert band that spring.

There were many things I picked up, and learned how important it was for individuals to work together as a team to get things accomplished. You might call it "sharing."

As you go through life you meet several types of people: the friends, the helpers, the motivators, and those who are positive. You will also meet or encounter several types of other people, like the critics, the naysayers, the jealous ones, along with those who really want to help or promote your ideas and what they stand for ... from the community at- large, as well as from various organizations you may be involved in.

Thank you goes out to the positive people who helped build a positive program.

– E.D.

THANKS FOR YOUR INSPIRATION

To all those individuals and boards, committees, trade groups, non-profit organizations, and government agencies, and so many who donated their time to our many projects, I THANK THEM ALL for the help and guidance they gave.

There were a variety of individuals at MSU who offered to help in the major you studied. They included presidents, vice-presidents, professors, or instructors, as the following:

John Hannah, President	Jack Breslin, Vice President
Fred Seibert	Herb Oyer
John Crawford	James Spaniolo
Erwin Bettinghaus	Ken Atkin
Frank Senger	Gordon Miracle
Gordon Sabine	Leo Deal
Leonard Falcone	Oscar Stover
Trajen Dubiel	Prabu David

Acknowledgements

In writing this book, there were many issues and activities which were related in the book. I have discussed ideas with several people that I know who have been part of our organizations such as my lovely wife, Joanne Deeb, Carol Cain, Marge Deeb, Michele Simon, John Ambrose, Walter Douglas, Harold Meeks, Chuck Stokes, Huel Perkins, Carmen Harlan, Fred Nahhat, John Minnis, John Prost, Lem Barney, Osama Siblani, Mayor Coleman A. Young, Jerry Blocker, and Tom Fox, etc.

I am glad that I decided to write this book because there are a lot of things in here people do not realize and that I hope will help them understand our important Detroit community.

Over the years, the Detroit area community has had its ups and downs. When our Nation was at war during World War II, we played a significant role while we were at war. The airplanes and tanks were built here and the military who played a key role included the Army, Navy, and Marines.

While there were many good times for us to talk about, there were things that were not so good. Such as, high unemployment at times, the rioting that took place in the 60's, and the lack of shopping facilities such as supermarkets, food markets, a need for more educational opportunities and so on.

But, due to all the positive things taking place in Detroit at the present time (2020), the area is growing rapidly. There are additional major companies who are coming in, more automobile assembly plants, much needed supermarkets and food stores to serve the people, more schooling and more opportunities for seniors and students. There is more I can add to this.

For those of you who are reading this book and have not been to Detroit recently, we encourage you to come back to Detroit to see how it has grown and how beautiful it has become.

Ed Deeb

ADDITIONAL HELPERS
ALONG THE WAY

ASSOCIATION
HELPERS

Louis Vescio

Phil Lauri

Harvey Weisberg

Jim Bonahoom

Don Harrington

Jim Vitale

Salman Sesi

Abe Michaels

Nabby Yono

Amir Denha

Don Criss

Hector Sossi

Ron Bedway

Carl Rashid

Dan Carmody

Mary Beth Ryan

Mona Gualtieri

Martha Reeves

Eric Wheelwright

Frank Gambino

Joanne Deeb

Marge Deeb

Ray Deeb

George Deeb

Beverly Smith

Jennifer Kluge

Jan Prevost

Nick Delich

Michele Simon

John Prost

Eric Maes

NaTasha Jones

John Neumann

Rich Woloch

MEDIA

The Detroit News

Detroit Free Press

Grosse Pointe News

Neal Shine

Carol Cain

Paul W. Smith

Peter Bhatia

Rich Homberg

Fred Nahhat

Mort Crim

Frank Angelo

Osama Siblani

Harold Meeks

Laydell Harper

Jonathan Wolman

Dick Puritan

Chuck Stokes

Devin Scillian

Huel Perkins

Marla Drutz

Carmen Harlan

Glenda Lewis

Bill Bonds

IN MEMORIAM

Raymond Deeb died in Sept. 2020 at his home in Grosse Pointe, MI. He was 82. Ray graduated from Southeastern High School in Detroit.

He worked at his parent's convenience store and at Jacobson's, Winkleman's and Albert's. He later taught autistic children at Grosse Pointe South and Grosse Pointe North High Schools.

Ray was very active in Metro Detroit Youth Day.

FORMULA FOR LIFE

Have a vision

Have a Purpose

Have a Passion

Have a good Attitude

Be a Climber

Let Teamwork make your Dreams Work

– Ed Deeb

SOME OF ED DEEB'S MEMORABLE ACCOMPLISHMENTS

<u>Michigan State University</u> – Founder, MSU College of Communication Arts Alumni Association and its first president

<u>Naming of room at MSU</u> – MSU named the College of Communication Arts conference room and lobby after him for all the work done at the brand new building at the University.

<u>Metro Detroit Youth Day</u> – Following altercations on Livernois Ave. in Detroit, Deeb played a key role in quelling the problem and working with Mayor Coleman A. Young of Detroit. Ed formed Metro Detroit Youth Day held at Belle Isle each year to inspire the youth to do the most good, instead of fighting and creating problems on the streets.

<u>Michigan Youth Appreciation Foundation</u> – 2 weeks later, Mr. Deeb formed the Michigan Youth Appreciation Foundation and reached out to all the high schools and youth organizations to participate in a huge big summer day full of attractive events. He also contacted all of the nearby colleges and universities in the area who began participating in the day at Belle Isle. This was a huge accomplishment and still goes on today.

<u>Food Dealers Assn. of Michigan</u> – In 1965, because of his journalism and public relations background, Ed Deeb was asked to become the CEO of the Food Dealers of Michigan,

replacing the person who retired. The organization grew from 95 members to 4,500 food companies, during his tenure.

<u>Michigan Food and Beverage Assn</u>. – In 1984, since Ed Deeb had created numerous programs for grocers, food processors, food manufacturers, food wholesalers, distributors, etc., he was encouraged to form the MFBA which he did. It grew from 0 to 6,000 members during his involvement.

<u>Assisting Media During the First Iraqi War</u> – When the first Iraqi war launched by the first president George H.W. Bush started, Mr. Deeb began receiving numerous calls from the news media asking who are the Iraqis?, who are the Chaldeans?, who are the Arabs? He graciously answered all questions to assist the news media, but it was taking a lot of his time so he decided to produce a video that would explain much of this. The video was titled "From A to Z, Arabic Contributions to the World." These were distributed to all major news media in Michigan – radio, television and newspapers – and later on to those media companies that wanted copies nationally. When the education community found out it was available, colleges, universities, high schools, libraries, etc. wanted copies of the videos. To date more than 2,200 copies of the video were distributed throughout the country.

ACCOMPLISHMENTS OF ED DEEB

Michigan State Lottery – Mr. Deeb noticed that many states were creating lotteries to generate funds for the state and the retailers, so he began calling for a lottery in Michigan. In 1971 former state senator, Gus Harrison, called Mr. Deeb and said he was ready to establish the lottery, but wanted Mr. Deeb to help convince his retail members to sell the tickets. The lottery began in 1972 and Mr. Deeb was asked to draw the first lottery ticket (991). In those days the lottery was $.50 once a week and didn't earn much revenue until later.

Historic Eastern Market – In 1972, Mr. Deeb received a call from various farmers and businesses in Eastern Market in Detroit. They were thinking of leaving the city because of the problems at the Market. They were having a meeting in one week and more than 20 merchants and farmers would be attending to complain that their businesses were getting no help from the City. Mr. Deeb attended the meeting and felt the frustration of these merchants and encouraged them not to leave the area. He said, "Let's keep it going for 3 more weeks to see if we can bring more activities to Eastern Market and more people to your establishments." As a result the Market grew.

Deeb organized parades down Russell Street by the Shriners and the Knights of Columbus, contests between churches and their gospel singers which drew 5-6 churches and brought more people to the Market. He then formed the Eastern Market Merchants Association to bring people together to find out what they wanted to see at the Market.

As a result, more people were coming to the Market and they started cooking contests and other activities at the Market.

Later, the Flower Growers Association at the Market asked Mr. Deeb to promote their organizations like he did with the Eastern Market farmers. So he did and 150 flower growers began being part of their association and on Saturdays the numbers grew from 30,000 to 70,000 people. He received the Lifetime Achievement Award for his efforts.

Assisting with the Problem at Ford Field – The security people at Ford Field contacted Ed Deeb two weeks before the first exhibition football game at the new stadium and said they were having problems with parking and the City would not let them park on the streets. They asked Mr. Deeb if he would call a meeting with the City since he was involved in Eastern Market, and let them park at Eastern Market during football games. He said he didn't know what he could do, but he would try. He contacted all the City groups in Detroit and said there was a dire need for parking during the football games and they wanted to be able to park at Eastern Market. After a two hour meeting, the City finally approved plans to have parking for football games at Eastern Market where they could walk to the stadium. This was a huge accomplishment for Ford Field, coordinated by Mr. Deeb.

Annual Holiday Food Baskets at Eastern Market – In 1985, Ed created a program to provide annual holiday food baskets for the senior citizens at Eastern Market. He received a call from the pastor of Sacred Heart Church in Eastern Market, Fr. Norman Thomas, who said the seniors in the area don't have any events, gifts, or food during the Christmas holiday. Mr. Deeb organized a program to encourage all the vendors in Eastern Market to donate food products one week before Christmas, and they were able to pack more than 300 major food baskets at Eastern Market for the senior citizens. Fr. Thomas and the seniors were very happy this occurred, and never stopped praising Mr. Deeb for his efforts even until today.

Receiving the Point of Light Award – In 1991, Mr. Deeb received a call from the White House stating that they wanted to present him with the newly formed Presidential Point of Light Award. When the secretary to President George H.W. Bush called, Mr. Deeb could not believe it was really a call from the President. She told hm it was, and that is why she was calling. The President invited Mr. Deeb and his wife to a special award presentation at Disney World and presented the medallion award to Mr. Deeb for all the work he has done in donating his time and efforts to the community of Detroit over the years. This was a very historic moment for Mr.Deeb, his family, and his members. It is one of the major awards he has received that he cherishes more than any others. Individuals from other states were also honored.

VARIOUS PHOTOS OF
ED DEEB, THE GO-TO-GUY

Founder Ed Deeb presents Michigan Gov. John Engler
with a special Metro Detroit Youth Day T-shirt

Michigan State University Alum
Ed Deeb poses with mascot, Sparty

Sam's Club, a major sponsor of Youth Day hosts an appreciation
breakfast for the Metro Detroit Youth Day committee

College & Professional team mascots pose on stage at Metro Youth Day

College Scholarship winners pose with their certificates at Metro Youth Day. More than 2,000 scholarships have been awarded.

Youngsters watching the entertainment on stage at Metro Detroit Youth Day

Ron Olson, Dept. of Natural Resources presents Ed Deeb with replica of street sign. A street on Belle Isle, Detroit was renamed in Deeb's name

Pictured in the photo include: Ed Deeb, Peter Bhatia, Detroit Free Press, and Chris Ilitch, Little Caesar's Pizza, Detroit Tigers and Detroit Red Wings.

Ed Deeb and other honorees of Detroit Public Schools pose for photo

MSU's John Ambrose and YD Scholarship coordinator
Speaks to crowd at Youth Day

Fox 2 WJBK reporter Roop Raj interviews Ed
Deeb on field at Belle Isle for Youth Day

Pres. George H.W. Bush presents Ed Deeb with the Point of Light
Medal with his wife, Joanne, looking on wife, Joanne looking on

Ed Deeb greets President Ronald Reagan on a visit to Michigan

Pictured left to right, Ed Deeb, President George Bush, and
Ed's daughter Jennifer Kluge, president of MBPA

Detroit Police Chief James Craig presents founder, Ed Deeb
with a proclamation at Metro Detroit Youth Day

Tellusdetroit, editor, Harold Meeks poses with
Distinguished Service Award at Youth Day event

Mayor and Detroit Piston, Dave Bing presents a proclamation
to Edward Deeb on stage at Metro Detroit Youth Day

Ed Deeb throws out the first pitch at the
Christmas in July Detroit Tigers game

Ronald McDonald mingles with the thousands
of kids at Metro Detroit Youth Day

Pictured on stage, left to right, Rochelle Riley, Nabby Yono,
Founder Ed Deeb, Martha Reeves, Hon. Martha Scott,
Dr. Jacoub Mansour, and Barbara Jean Johnsn

Dave Bing, L. Brooks Patterson. Robert Ficano,
& Ed Deeb pose for the photographer

Youth Day sponsors pose for picture. L to R, Ed Deeb, Tony
Michaels, Hon. Barbara McQuade and Gerard Anderson

Pictured at Thanksgiving Parade Pancake Breakfast, L to R, Dan
Loepp, BCBSM, Paul W. Smith, WJR Radio, Tony Michaels, The
Parade Co. and Edward Deeb, founder Metro Edtroit Youth Day

Ralph Nader, center, Ralph Bahna, right, and Ed Deeb at a reception in Washington DC.

Macomb County, Michigan Executive, Mark Hackel, poses with John Prost, left and Ed Deeb at the kick-off breakfast for the Detroit Thanksgiving Parade

Detroit Lions and Hall of Famer, Lem Barney, left, poses for a photograph with Chairman Ed Deeb at an appreciation breakfast

Governor of Michigan, Jim Blanchard, center, is pictured with Ed Deeb, left, and radio personality Dick Purtan at a Salvation Army reception.

Columnist and Business Leader, George Deeb

Ed's lovely wife, Joanne, left, and Ed, right pose for a photograph at a dinner reception,

The Bridge Builder

An old man going along the highway
Came in the evening, cold and gray.
To a chasm vast, both deep and wide,
The old man crossed in the twilight dim;
The swollen stream was as naught to him;
But he stopped when safe on the farther side
And built a bridge to span the tide.

"Old man," said a fellow pilgrim near,
"You are wasting your strength in labor here;
Your journey will end with the closing day,
You never again will pass this way.
You've crossed the chasm deep and wide
Why build you this bridge at eventide?"

The laborer lifted his old gray head,
"Good friend, in the path I have come," he said,
"There followeth after me today
A youth whose feet must pass this way.
This chasm which has been naught to me
To that young man may a pitfall be.
He, too, must cross in the twilight dim.
Good friend, I am building this bridge for him."

– Miss Will Allen Dromgoole

Printed in the United States
by Baker & Taylor Publisher Services